All about you

Where did you come from?

Jillian Powell

Wayland

All *about you*

Where did you come from?
Who are you?
Who are your family?
Who are your friends?

Picture acknowledgements

The publishers would like to thank the following for allowing their photographs to be reproduced in this book: Reflections (Jennie Woodcock) *frontispiece*, 4, 17 (above), 20 (both), 22 (above), 24 (both); Science Photo Library 7 (Francis Leroy/Biocosmos), 8 (Petit Format/Nestle), 10 (all/Petit Format/Nestle), 11 (Larry Mulvehill), 14 (Simon Fraser), 16 (below/Larry Mulvehill), 21 (Chris Priest); Tony Stone Worldwide 25 (Andy Cox), 26 (Andy Cox), 28 (Jo Browne/Mick Smee); Tim Woodcock Photo Library *cover*, 9; ZEFA 5, 8, 15, 16 (above), 18, 22 (below), 23, 27.

Editor: Francesca Motisi
Series designer: Jean Wheeler

First published in 1993 by
Wayland (Publishers) Limited
61, Western Road, Hove
East Sussex, BN3 1JD England

British Cataloguing in Publication Data

Powell, Jillian
Where did you come from – (All About You Series)
I. Title   II. Series
612.6

ISBN 0-7502-0731-0

Typeset by Dorchester Typesetting Group Limited
Printed and bound by G. Canale and C.S.p.A., Turin, Italy

Contents

You began life as a baby.
You are made of lots of tiny,
living bits called **cells**.

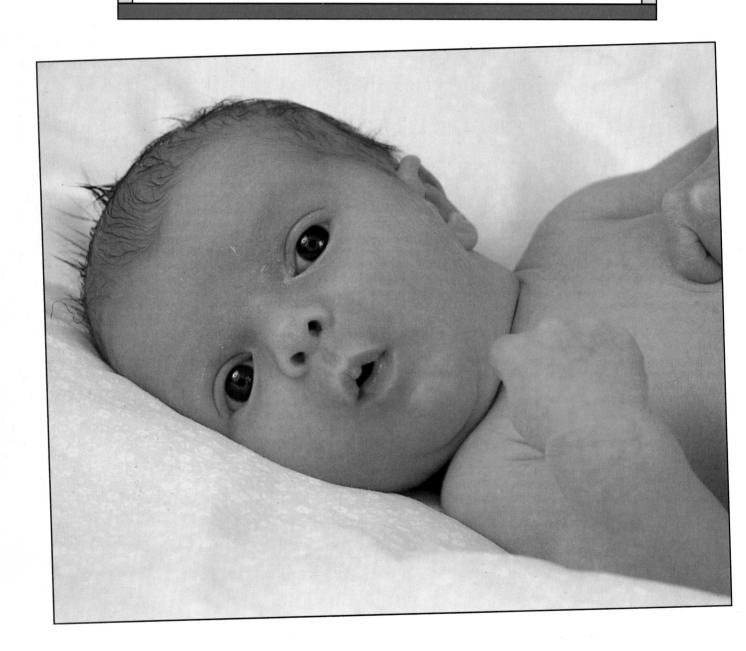

You were made by a man and a woman.

You began life when your parents were having **sex**.

Your dad put his penis inside your mum's vagina and sperm cells went from his penis into your mum's body.

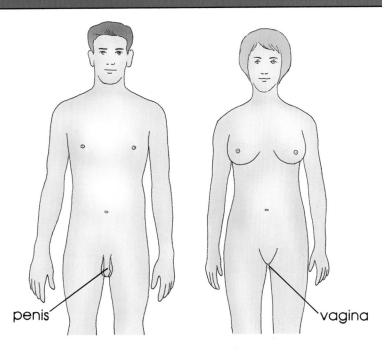

penis

vagina

Then an egg cell from your mum and a sperm cell from your dad joined inside your mum's body to make a new cell.

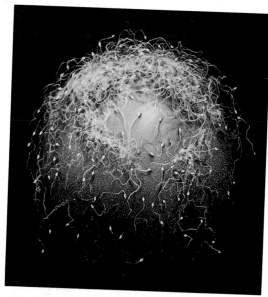

sperm cells surrounding an egg cell

7

The new cell began to grow in your mum's **womb**, the place where babies grow.

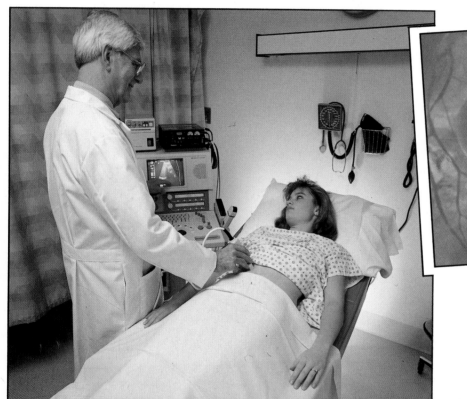

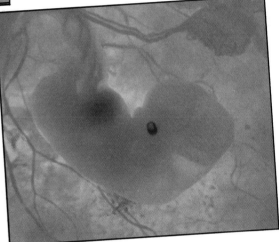

embryo

The cell grew into an **embryo**, the start of a baby – the start of you! The doctor checked on a special machine to make sure you and your mum were both healthy.

As you continued to grow your
mum's tummy grew bigger
to make room for the baby
inside her.

After a few weeks, your heart was beating, you had eyes, ears, arms and legs and you began to move.

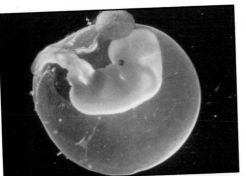

Embryo at six weeks.

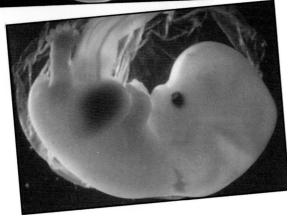

Embryo at seven weeks.

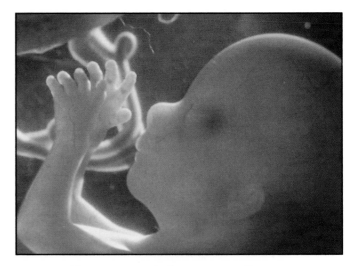

Embryo at four months.

A special cord joined you to your mother's womb, bringing you the food and air you needed to grow.

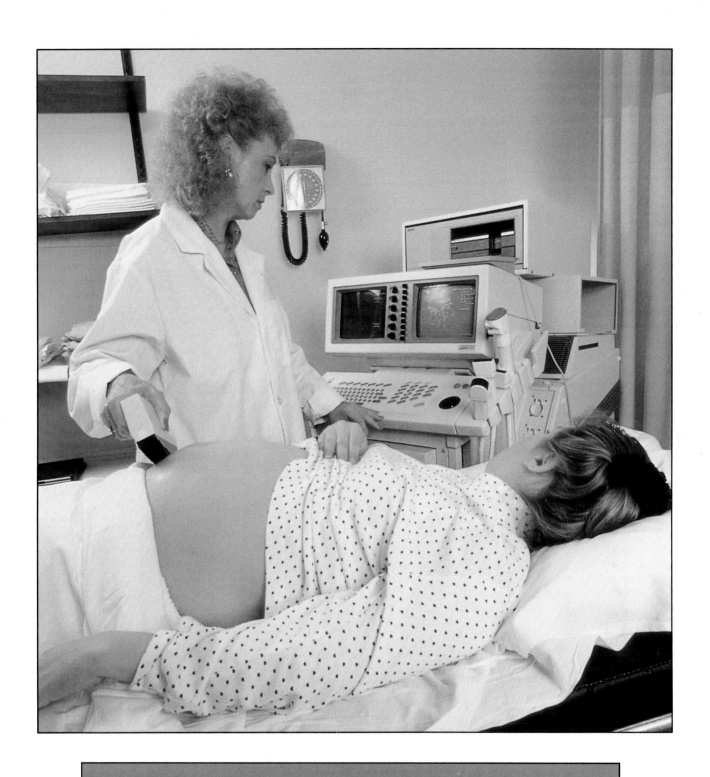

The doctor checked again on the special machine to make sure you were healthy.

After six months you looked like this. You could move your arms about and kick your legs.

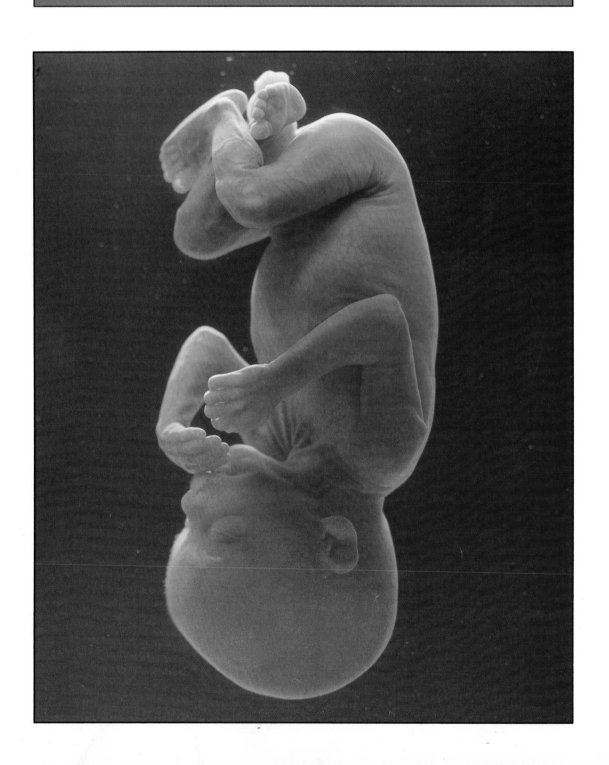

After six months your mum
looked like this. Sometimes she
could feel you kicking inside her.

It took about forty weeks until you were ready to be born. The doctor made sure your mum was healthy before you were born.

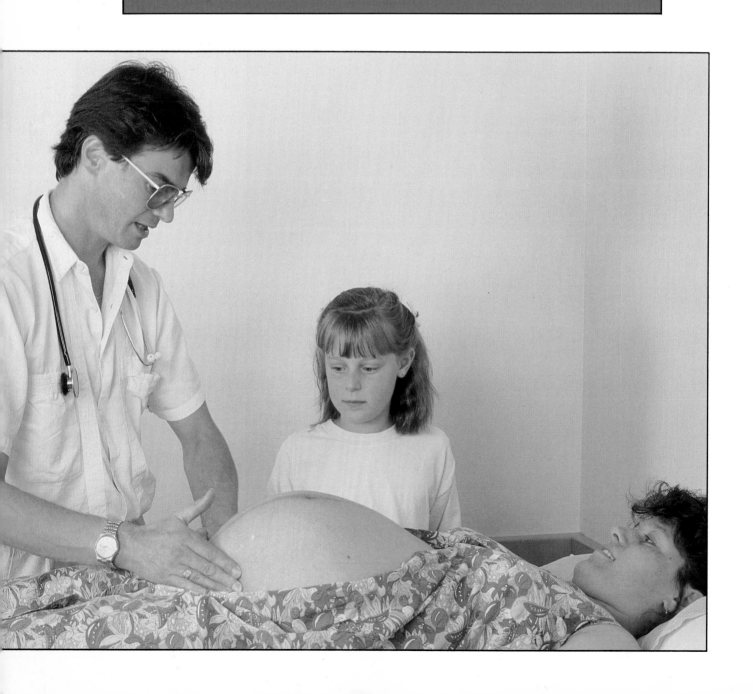

You may have been born in hospital or at home. A doctor and nurses probably helped your mum give birth. It was hard work for her!

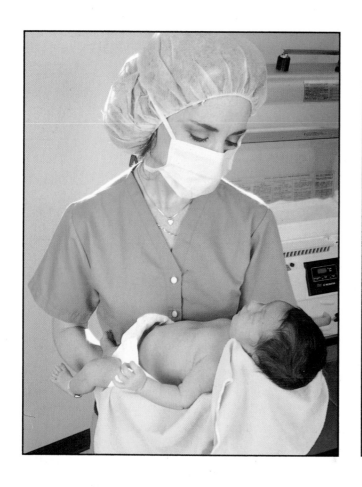

After you were born, a nurse cut the cord that joined you to your mother. Your tummy button is where your cord was.

You took your first breaths into your **lungs**.

Your dad probably came to see you in hospital. He may have brought your older brother or sister to see you and your mum.

When you were first born a doctor weighed and measured you at the hospital.

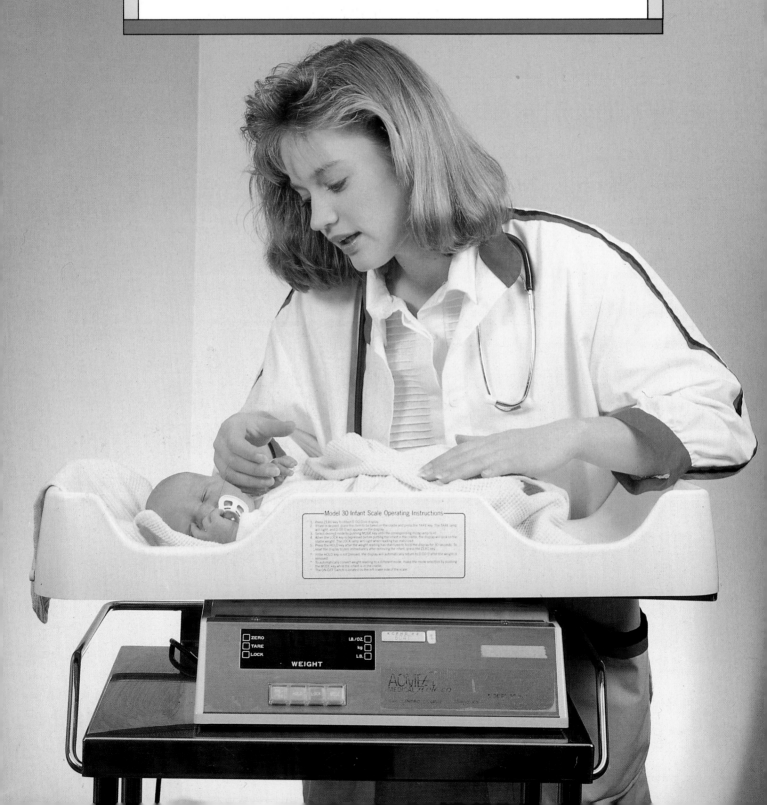

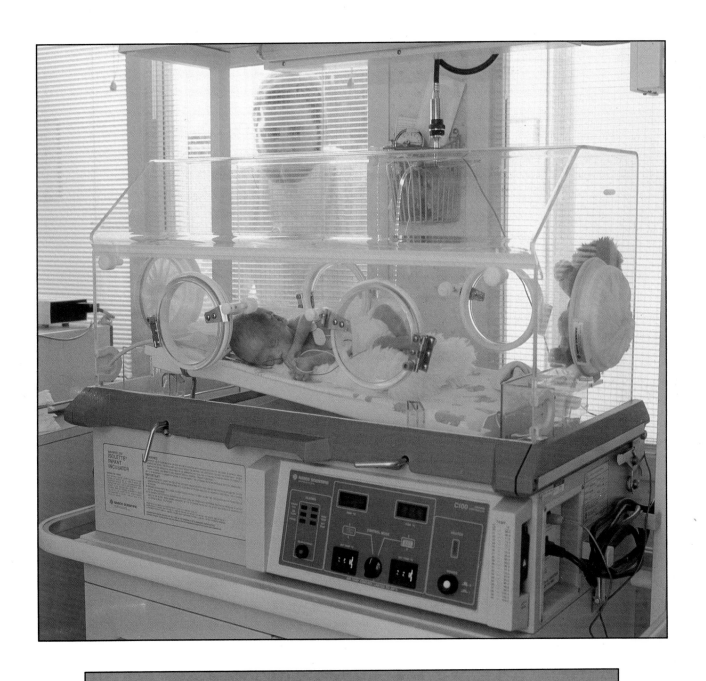

Some babies are born too
early and need special care
to help them put on weight
and grow.

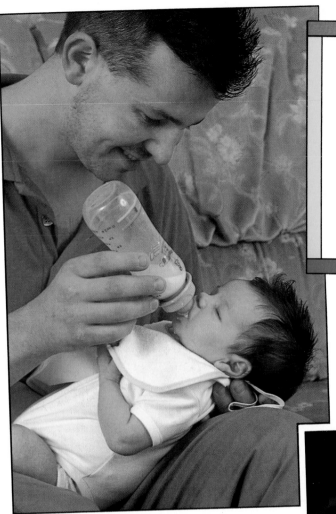

You needed milk to help you grow. You may have been fed by bottle.

Or you may have been fed milk from your mother's breast.

After a few months your mum
stopped giving you milk and
you began to eat special
baby food.

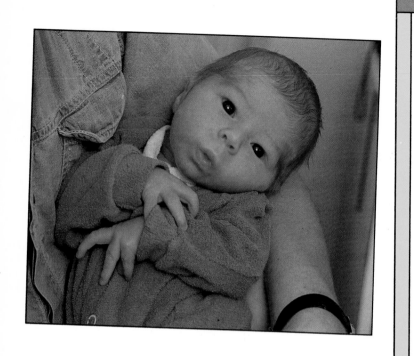

When you were first born you were floppy and couldn't hold your head up on your own. Later you grew strong enough to hold your head up.

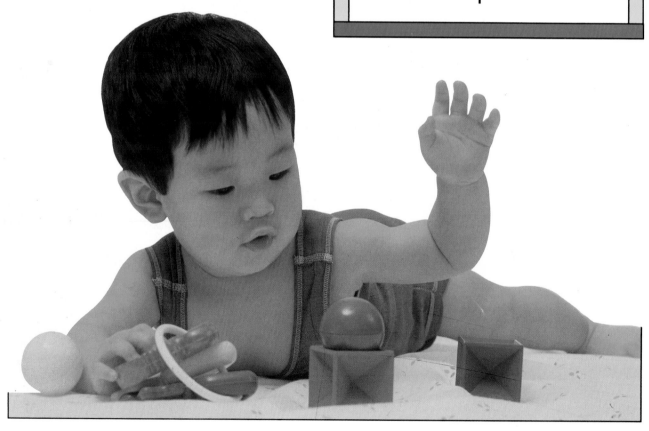

You kept growing stronger and bigger until you could sit up on your own.

After about nine months you learned to crawl.

At first you needed help when you tried to walk.

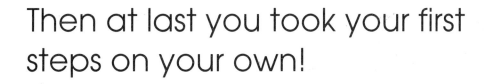

Then at last you took your first steps on your own!

You learned to talk by copying the sounds people around you made.

At first, you just made noises, then you learned to say your first words.

As you grew, your **brain** and your **five senses** helped you learn new things.

You began to think about the world around you. You were becoming you.

Notes for parents and teachers

Maths
● Data handling: collect data on children's birth weights and express graphically e.g. in a bar chart.
● Symmetry: (see Art).
● Number work/sets: e.g. sort into sets animals that suckle (mammals); lay eggs; help to rear their young etc.

Language
● Collect the names given to the young of various creatures – link to a discussion of collective nouns.
● Creative writing: metamorphosis – imagine waking up one morning as some other creature.
● Story: Read/make up their own versions of books such as: *The Very Hungry Caterpillar, Ah! Said Stork, The Tiny Seed, The Bad Baby* etc.

Science
● Life cycles: a) plants (seeds, labelling parts of a plant and identifying those parts involved in reproduction); b) creatures: (including the metamorphosis of frogs, butterflies etc.), c) people.
● Reproduction: plants, animals, people.
● Mammals: investigation into what constitutes a mammal – unusual examples like the egg-laying platypus.
● A study of the conditions needed to sustain life (see Health).

Technology
● In small groups or individually, children could devise a dice game which involves players taking a journey in the form of a life-story or life cycle. Plan, make, evaluate, formulate possible improvements.

Geography
● Study of the seasons and how these relate to the life cycles of plants and animals. Investigation into those countries which have no/different seasons.
● Child-rearing practices in other countries: clothes and costumes and how these relate to climate and custom.

History
● A general discussion and investigation into the effect of progress in medicine and health could touch on how the infant mortality rate has been improved by vaccination etc.
● Family trees.

Art and Craft
● Symmetrical pictures/paintings e.g. 'butterfly' prints created by folding paper.
● Pictorial representations, or models using plasticine or papier mâché, of animal life cycles.

PE/Dance/Drama
● Children could be encouraged to explore a range of large apparatus in three ways, reflecting the stages of development of a child: a) crawling, b) walking, c) walking and climbing.
● Guided fantasy.
● Children could act out or devise their own dance to reflect the stages in the life of a person from birth to old-age and death, or the life cycle of a frog or butterfly.

Music
● Listening to and appreciating appropriate pieces of music e.g. Vivaldi's *Four Seasons* Stravinsky's *Rite of Spring*.
● Singing songs: there is a great deal of material which has birth/rebirth as its theme.
● Compositions which reflect the life-story themes of birth and death.

Multicultural/RE./Health
● Conditions that are needed to sustain life (see Science).
● People who help us: at home, at school, in society.
● Child-rearing customs and practices in different countries e.g. Sikh birth ceremony may express the hope that the baby will grow up to serve others; some African people bring the new born baby out into the night and hold her/him up to the sky.
● 'Beginnings': a discussion of the various 'creation myths' from various countries and religions.

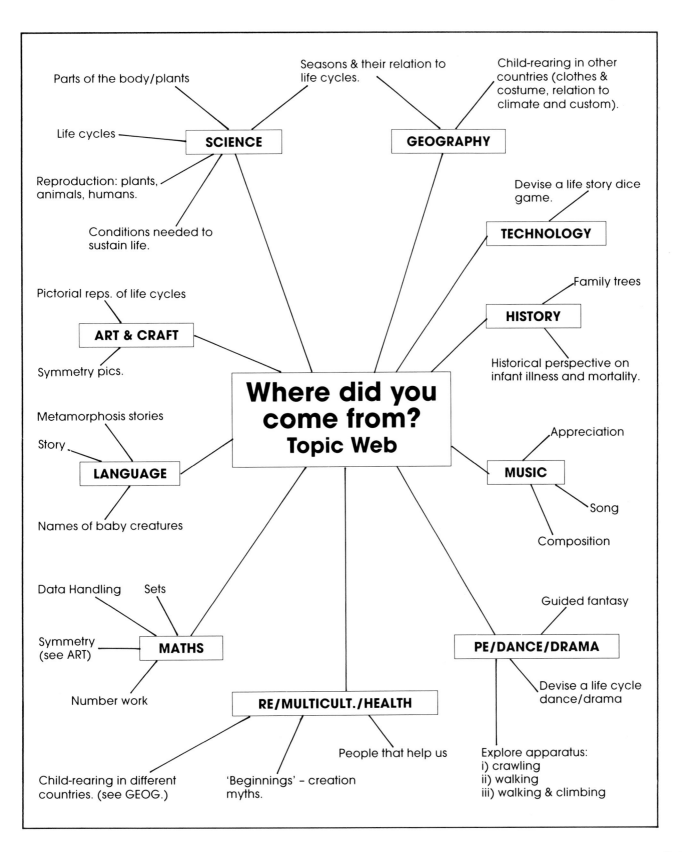

Parts of the body/plants

Seasons & their relation to life cycles.

Child-rearing in other countries (clothes & costume, relation to climate and custom).

Life cycles ── **SCIENCE**

GEOGRAPHY

Reproduction: plants, animals, humans.

Conditions needed to sustain life.

Devise a life story dice game.

TECHNOLOGY

Family trees

Pictorial reps. of life cycles

HISTORY

ART & CRAFT

Historical perspective on infant illness and mortality.

Symmetry pics.

Where did you come from?
Topic Web

Metamorphosis stories

Appreciation

Story

MUSIC

LANGUAGE

Song

Names of baby creatures

Composition

Data Handling   Sets

Guided fantasy

Symmetry (see ART) ── **MATHS**

PE/DANCE/DRAMA

Number work

Devise a life cycle dance/drama

RE/MULTICULT./HEALTH

People that help us

Explore apparatus:
i) crawling
ii) walking
iii) walking & climbing

Child-rearing in different countries. (see GEOG.)

'Beginnings' – creation myths.

Glossary

Brain The part of the body in your head with which you think.
Cell The smallest living part of a body or plant.
Embryo The name given to a baby during the first two months of growth in the womb.
Five senses Hearing, sight, smell, taste and touch.
Lungs The part of the body body with which you breathe.
Sex Short for sexual intercourse – when two people make love to give each other pleasure and sometimes to make babies.
Womb The part of a woman's body in which a baby grows.

Index

Books to read

Where Do Babies Come From? – Susan Meredith (Usborne 1991)

The Birds And The Bees – Sue Baker (Child's Play 1990)

How A Baby Is Made – Per Holm Knudsen (Piccolo Books 1975)

Where Do Babies Come From? (Invader 1992)